D0572702

A DAY THAT MADE HISTORY

HIROSHIMA

Stephen Hoare

Dryad Press Limited   London

Contents

Acknowledgments

The author and publishers thank the following for their kind permission to reproduce copyright photographs: Associated Press Ltd, pages 3, 24 (bottom), 54, 62; BBC Hulton Picture Library, pages 30, 53; *Chugoku-Shimbum*, page 25; Shigeo Hayashi, page 27; Hiroshima/Nagasaki Publishing Committee, page 26; Robert Hunt Library, pages 47, 48; Imperial War Museum, pages 8, 24 (top), 42; The Photo Source, title page, pages 6, 16-17, 20, 21, 22, 28, 29 (US Navy), 38, 44, 45, 46, 55, 56; The Research House Pictures, pages 11 (US Army Air Forces Photo), 19 (UN Photo), 61; Topham Photo Library, page 40; UPI/Bettmann Newsphotos, pages 13, 53, 59. The maps on pages 4-5 and the diagrams on pages 31, 44-45 are by R.F. Brien. The pictures were researched by David Pratt.

Cover photograph: The centre of Hiroshima photographed by the US Army after the surrender of Japan (US Army photo).

The "Day that Made History" series was devised by Nathaniel Harris.

© Stephen Hoare 1987. First published 1987.
Typeset by Tek-Art Ltd, Kent, and printed by R.J. Acford, Chichester, Sussex
for the publishers, Dryad Press Limited, 8 Cavendish Square, London W1M 0AJ

ISBN 0 8521 9695 4

THE
EVENTS

Hiroshima: 6th August, 1945

Hiroshima today

The early morning rush-hour traffic roars. Businessmen in suits hurry to work in the skyscraper offices of this thriving commercial centre. On the streets, neon signs and posters advertize Coca Cola and Nissan cars. Looking up at the tall concrete and glass buildings, you could be in any city in the world. But this is Hiroshima, the eighth largest city in Japan.

In the centre is a small park. Green lawns surround the ruins of the city's oldest building. But these ruins are not of smooth stone or of mellow brick; they are jagged concrete and steel – all that remains of the former Industry Promotion

The skeleton of the Industry Promotion Centre building has been preserved as a memorial. It is at the centre of the rebuilt city of Hiroshima.

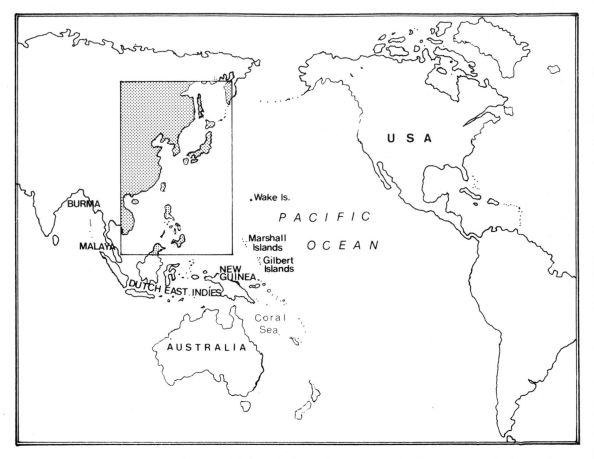

Centre. This reinforced concrete shell was one of the only structures left standing when Hiroshima was destroyed by the world's first atomic bomb on 6th August, 1945.

Near the ruins is a small museum and one of its most telling exhibits is the half-melted remains of a lady's wrist-watch. The hands on the dial point to 8.16 a.m.

*　　*　　*　　*　　*　　*　　*

In the closing days of the Second World War, Japan was a nation under siege. The US navy and airforce were operating a tight blockade on all shipping entering or leaving Japan's ports. Mass bombing raids carried out by American long-range bombers were reducing Japanese cities to rubble, one by one. As an important port and industrial centre, the city of Hiroshima was under threat of destruction.

Hiroshima lies on the southern coast of Honshu, Japan's largest island. In ancient times the city was founded on an

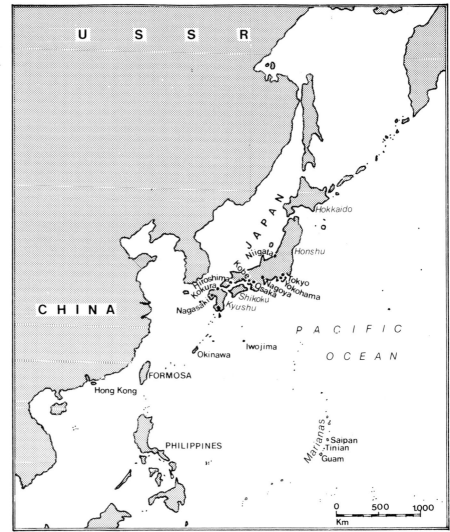

island in the middle of the delta formed by the Ohta river – the name Hiroshima means "broad island". The delta's six wide channels made a natural defensive moat and the warriors of Japan's feudal past evidently appreciated Hiroshima's military value for in the late fourteenth century a local warlord built a castle on the island. Its stone walls rose steeply from the river bank. Hiroshima's early defenders would have looked out across the flat plain to the north and the sea to the south, and the people of the city would thus have had early warning of an attack.

In 1945 the castle offered no defence against Japan's latest enemy. The city had spread beyond its early confines, to cover the entire delta, and the Ohta's sluggish channels, no barrier to modern land forces, were now criss-crossed by many bridges. Nonetheless, the tradition of Hiroshima castle lived on. In 1945 the Japanese army walked its ramparts and the picturesque old castle was a part of the headquarters of the Second General Army.

Hiroshima was one of Japan's biggest and most important military bases. Barracks, parade grounds, administrative buildings and supply dumps occupied large areas of the city. Altogether, about 100,000 army personnel were stationed there.

Besides the troops, the castle was host to twenty-three American airmen. The men, who had formed the crews of two B29 bombers recently shot down, were locked in their cells, waiting to face another day of tough questioning. Their captors viewed them as beneath contempt, for by tradition Japanese soldiers preferred death to the dishonour of surrender and the motto of the Japanese army was: "Our highest hope is to die for the Emperor".

The Japanese knew they were losing the war. Many of them must have had members of their families killed in the terrible incendiary bombing raids that had burnt to the ground cities like Tokyo, Yokohama, Nagoya, Kobe and Osaka. Perhaps some of the soldiers wondered when it would be Hiroshima's turn to become a victim of the "B-San" – "Mr B", as the

B29 bombers over Mount Fuji.

Japanese wryly called the dreaded B29. So far, Hiroshima had escaped with only two very light raids on its outskirts.

Outside the castle, the citizens of Hiroshima were waking up and preparing for the hard toil of the day ahead. 6th August, like the previous day, had dawned cloudless and bright. It was one of the last truly hot summer days before the skies would cloud over, heralding the start of the rainy season.

It had been an eventful night. The city had been on the alert after two air-raid warnings. People had been woken by the klaxons and had taken shelter in the improvised holes in the ground that the authorities had instructed civilians to build. For the most part, these shelters were shallow pits beneath the floors of houses. Twice, formations of "B-San" had flown over the city, and twice the "all-clear" had sounded when the danger had passed. No bombs had fallen and the city awakened to face a fresh day . . . .

Susumu Kimura, a fourteen-year-old student at the Hiroshima Prefectural Girls' High School, had risen early to help prepare the family's breakfast with her mother. In spite of the night's disturbances she was excited and looking forward to this day. She was going with her older sister to visit relatives in the country. For both girls it would mean a brief holiday from the unrelenting toil of daily life when days spent in the classroom were followed by days spent on community work projects, according to official decree. Community work could mean working in one of the city's munition factories or taking part in a civil defence project, for instance, being trained to use the bamboo spears with which, it was intended, Japan's entire population should defend their country to the very last drop of their blood. Time spent in school was governed by a strict rotation of power cuts, which also closed each of the local factories in turn. Raw materials, power and food were all rationed as Japan strained to muster every last part of her dwindling resources for the American invasion that everyone thought was coming.

Susumu's father left for his office in the city centre at about 7.30 a.m. At ten minutes to eight, the ominous sound of an air-raid klaxon filled the air. With her mother and sister, Susumu climbed down into their shallow shelter beneath a *tatami* mat spread on the living-room floor. The American planes passed high overhead. Ten minutes later the "all-clear" sounded and family life returned slowly to normal.

Shortly after eight, Susumu's sister left the house. She had

These typical Japanese wooden houses survived the explosion because they were protected by a valley.

one last morning to complete with a work party which had been raised to help prepare the city for the expected bombing attacks. Much of Hiroshima consisted of one- or two-storey wooden houses, closely packed together. The city's civil defence chiefs had realized there would be little chance of stopping fire spreading rapidly, in the event of an incendiary bombing raid. Susumu's sister was a member of a team which had been given the job of demolishing rows of houses, to make fire-breaks.

Susumu and her mother started to clear away the breakfast things. They heard the sound of planes overhead. The time was 8.15 . . . .

Soon after the "all-clear" sounded at 8.00, the radio news reported several B29s in the area of Hiroshima, but said they were probably reconnaissance planes. Since Japan had lost most of her airforce, the American planes could come and go unchallenged. They made frequent flights over Japan to photograph the effects of bombing raids and to make aerial surveys. There was never any danger from these planes as they flew over in ones or twos, and the Japanese people accepted them as one of the minor irritations of daily life . . . .

Tatsuko Mori waved goodbye to her husband as he left for work at 7 a.m. as usual. She lived with her husband, parents-in-law and elder son, aged two, in a traditional wooden house in the middle-class residential district of Ushita. Tatsuko had left her younger son with her parents in the country. Most young children had been evacuated to the countryside, but Tatsuko could not bear to be parted from her first child.

Although they were reasonably well-off, the Mori family had no more than the same meagre rations that were allowed every family in Japan. To feed her family, Tatsuko was given 30 grammes of dried bread and three to four cupfuls of poor-quality rice or soya beans a day. Three or four times a month, each family was given a bundle of noodles and, by saving up their ration cards, families could also look forward to a few fresh vegetables, bean curd and possibly one small fish in the course of a week.

That morning, Tatsuko strapped her child to her back and left the house with her elderly father-in-law. They were setting out in the direction of a local village to forage for edible wild plants and roots. They were not alone in this search. Hunger had forced many of the citizens of Hiroshima to go seeking anything remotely edible that could be added to their diet. Wild birds were netted and people put baited hollow bamboo traps in the river, to catch eels.

At about 8.14 Tatsuko pointed to a group of three planes in the distance. Why were they there? The "all-clear" had sounded before she and her father-in-law had left home. As they looked up, one of the planes detached itself from the group and flew over the city centre. An object dropped from it and a small parachute billowed open. The low droning quickly turned to a high-pitched roar as the plane banked steeply away towards the sea. The sun shone momentarily on its exposed fuselage, the shining metal reflecting the sun's rays.

The tiny parachute and the object suspended below it came slowly earthwards. Tatsuko and her father-in-law stared up at it. The time was a few seconds to 8.16.

The *Enola Gay*

Tinian is a small coral island at the southern end of the Marianas chain. These islands are the peaks of an underwater mountain range which rises more than six miles from the bed of the Pacific Ocean. In August 1944 US marines made an assault on Tinian and, after a prolonged and bloody battle, managed to dislodge its Japanese defenders from their heavily fortified positions. Saipan and Guam, larger islands in the same chain, fell at around the same time. Altogether, 42,000 Japanese soldiers and 5,000 Americans were killed. The American capture of the Marianas, 1,500 miles south of the Japanese home islands, brought Japan's cities within range of the world's heaviest plane, the B29 superfortress bomber. The final chapter in Japan's defeat was about to begin.

Immediately, construction teams began the task of flattening palm trees and coral to make way for a huge airforce base and a system of roads that would grow to occupy about half of Tinian's 39 square miles. Four parallel runways were planned, running from one side of the tiny island to the other. By December 1944 one runway, North Field, was in operation. Bombing missions against Japan started soon afterwards.

*   *   *   *   *   *   *

At fifteen minutes past midnight on 6th August, 1945, the long, low bulk of a superfortress bomber stood in readiness at the end of its runway on Tinian. A man in overalls approached. It was the bomber's flight engineer, Staff Sergeant Wyatt Duzenbury, about to begin his routine pre-flight inspection. Tonight, Duzenbury would spend two hours, exhaustively checking the mechanical controls, the instruments, the wiring circuits and the engines. He knew he was going on a very special mission. As he neared the bomber's nose, Duzenbury looked up and noted that the plane's new nickname, *Enola Gay*, had been painted just below the cockpit. Enola Gay was the maiden name of the pilot's mother.

While Duzenbury made his inspection, Colonel Paul Tibbets, pilot of the *Enola Gay*, and his crew were dining in the group's mess hut. With them were the crews of the five other planes that would all play a vital part in the coming operation. Three B29s would leave ahead of the *Enola Gay*,

The Enola Gay *stands on the runway of Tinian airforce base.*

to report on weather conditions over the cities that had been selected as possible targets. The primary target was Hiroshima, but if the city was covered in clouds, the attack could be switched elsewhere at the last moment.

Two B29s would accompany the *Enola Gay*, carrying cameras and scientific equipment to record the destructive effect of the atom bomb. Clear skies were essential for the mission; there was no room for mistakes. Besides aiming the bomb accurately, it was important to obtain clear photographs of the explosion and its aftermath.

The bombers' crews were all members of the 509th Composite Group, an elite squadron that had been assigned a special role outside the routine of a normal airforce bomber group. Instead of being sent on active service, they had been kept in the United States. From their base in the Utah desert they had taken part in training missions, dropping strange-shaped dummy bombs on target, with pin-point accuracy and from a great height. Stranger than that, pilots had had to practise making tight, 155-degree turns away from the ground target area, an aerobatic manoeuvre more suited to a fighter than to a heavy bomber.

Since their arrival on the island the men of the 509th had been separated from the rest of the base by a high wire security fence. They had not been on any dangerous missions and had suffered no losses. The battle-hardened crews outside 509's compound often hurled insults at the men on the other side of the fence. But in the early hours of the morning of 6th August 509 Group knew that at last they faced the mission for which they had been trained.

Two days earlier, Tibbets had received word that, for the next forty-eight hours, weather conditions over Hiroshima would be ideal. He had been briefed on the intended raid and on the exact nature of the bomb he would be carrying by no less a person than General Tooey Spaatz, overall Commander of Airforces in the Pacific. Spaatz himself was acting on the direct authority of the President of the United States, Harry S. Truman.

As soon as Tibbets had received the go-ahead from Spaatz, he had summoned his air crews for an immediate briefing. After giving details of the target, the timing of the operation and the planes that would be taking part, Tibbets introduced Captain William Parsons, a naval bomb expert who would be joining him on the flight. Parsons told the men something about the special bomb they would be carrying. "The bomb you are going to drop," he said, "is something new in the history of warfare. It is the most destructive ever produced. We think it will knock out everything within a three mile area." He then showed them film of the testing of the first atomic bomb at Alamogordo, New Mexico. There were gasps of disbelief. No mention was made of the fact that the bomb, code-named "Little Boy", was atomic.

The men finished eating and were called to duty. At 1.37 a.m. the three weather planes took off for Japan. The destination of the first, *Straight Flush*, piloted by Captain Claude Eatherley, was Hiroshima. The other planes headed for the cities of Niigata, Kokura and Nagasaki, secondary targets that had been chosen in case Hiroshima was obscured by cloud.

About an hour later, Colonel Tibbets and his crew posed for a photograph under the glare of floodlights, before entering their aircraft. Once inside, they began making routine pre-flight checks on all the instruments. Tibbets had every confidence in his plane and in his crew – he had chosen them personally. He particularly valued the ability of his navigator, Theo Van Kirk, to predict to within seconds their time of arrival over the target. He knew, too, that his bombardier, Major Thomas Ferebee, could drop a bomb with more accuracy than any other member of the group. From a height of 9,000 metres, he was never more than 100 metres from the aiming point.

As Tibbets ran through his instrument checks, Sergeant Duzenbury, the flight engineer, made his report. Gauges showed that the fuel tanks had been loaded to maximum capacity – 31,000 litres, enough to make Japan and back.

Some of the ground crew, with Paul Tibbets in the centre, pictured here on the Enola Gay's return to Tinian.

Tibbets fired the engines and ran them slowly. He held the brakes on.

Meanwhile, Captain Parsons and his assistant, Lieutenant Morris Jeppson, were checking the single 4½-tonne bomb that sat in the middle of the *Enola Gay*'s specially adapted bomb bay. For Parsons, the most dangerous part of the mission would be the hours immediately following take-off. It was then that he planned to assemble the bomb's conventional explosive charge and detonator. Dangerous as this task may have appeared, it was much safer to assemble the bomb in the air than to allow the plane to take off with a live atom bomb on board. An accident at that critical time – and there had been several crashes on the base's runways – would certainly detonate the bomb.

From the cockpit, Tibbets spoke to his crew members through an intercom. Was everything prepared? At exactly 2.45 a.m., the message came from Tinian's control tower telling Tibbets that the *Enola Gay* was cleared for take-off.

Zero hour

When he received clearance for take-off Tibbets nodded to his co-pilot, Robert Lewis. "Let's go." Tibbets released the brakes and pushed the throttle forward, gunning the four huge 2,200 h.p. propeller engines into life. The plane gradually picked up speed until it reached the end of the 2,590-metre runway which jutted out over the seashore. Tibbets had been holding the plane down to ensure maximum speed for take-off. At the very last moment, he pulled back the stick and the plane was airborne.

It had been a tense moment and Ferebee, whose seat was in the plane's plexiglass nose below the pilot, must have felt relieved as they rose slowly above the dark and tranquil Pacific Ocean. Sitting behind the pilot, Theo Van Kirk, the navigator, began plotting a north-westerly course towards Hiroshima. The *Enola Gay*'s flight path would take it above the island of Iwojima. Iwojima had fallen to the Americans and on its recently completed airstrip another B29 stood ready to take over from the *Enola Gay* if any mechanical faults developed along the way.

A few minutes after take-off, Parsons and his assistant crawled through a narrow passage leading to the belly of the aircraft, where "Little Boy" was awaiting attention. The restricted space inside the bomb bay was poorly lit and, to make matters worse, it was neither still nor quiet – these were not the ideal conditions to start tampering with an atom bomb, the equivalent of 20,000 tonnes of TNT! Parsons, however, was confident. He had spent hours assembling and dismantling the bomb's detonator and conventional explosive charge, both before and after "Little Boy" had been winched into the specially converted bomb bay. Despite its name, "Little Boy" was 3 metres long and practically filled the area.

Parsons placed his tool box on the catwalk beside the bomb. In it were a pair of pliers, a set of screwdrivers and some wrenches. While he got down to work, Jeppson stood behind him with a flashlight. It did not take long to place the detonator in position. Then Parsons began wiring up the bomb's firing circuits. For safety's sake, all the bomb's fuses had been de-activated. When he had finished, Parsons placed a detector box beside the bomb to monitor its level of radioactivity. If the bomb ever became unstable, the red light on the box would start flashing and the bomb would have to be jettisoned. Parsons and his assistant took turns to watch the box for the rest of the flight. Later they would set the fuses that would make the bomb "live".

While Parsons and Jeppson worked, the *Enola Gay* and its two escorting planes kept a steady course towards Iwojima. The crew of the *Enola Gay* went about their duties quietly and the atmosphere on board was almost relaxed. There was no danger from the enemy as, by this stage of the war, US forces had the upper hand at sea and in the air.

At about 4.30 a.m. Tibbets handed over the controls to his co-pilot and came to visit the crew. He crawled through the narrow passageway past the bomb bay to the plane's mid-section, where the radar observers and two gunners sat. Tibbets chatted and joked with the men. He also spoke to his tail gunner, Robert Caron:

> "Bob, have you figured out what we are doing this morning?" Tibbets asked.
> "Colonel, I don't want to get put up against a wall and shot," the gunner said nervously.
> Tibbets grinned at him. "We are on the way now. You can talk."
> "Are we carrying a chemists' nightmare?" Caron asked.
> "No, not exactly."
> "How about a physicists' nightmare?"
> "Yes."
> Tibbets turned to go. Caron tugged at his leg.
> "What's the problem?" he said looking over his shoulder.
> "No problem, colonel. Just a question. Are we splitting atoms?"
> (Quoted in Keith Wheeler, *The Fall of Japan*, Time-Life Books, 1983)

At 5.05 a.m. the *Enola Gay* and its escort planes flew over Iwojima in loose formation. Tibbets exchanged a few words with ground control of the airforce base below. The stand-by plane waiting on the airstrip would not be needed. The three bombers continued north-westward towards Japan.

At about 6.30 a.m. Parsons and Jeppson finally armed the bomb, replacing the three red plugs in its fuses with three green ones. They left the bomb bay, closing its airtight door behind them, and joined the crew in the mid-section. The *Enola Gay* was about to begin its long and steady climb to bombing altitude – 9,000 metres.

Before starting the climb, Tibbets switched on his intercom

and made an important announcement to the crew. "We are carrying the world's first atomic bomb. When the bomb is dropped, Beser [the radio officer] will record your reactions. This recording is for history, so watch your language . . . . Now we're going to start climbing." What Tibbets did not tell the crew was that in his pocket he carried a packet of cyanide

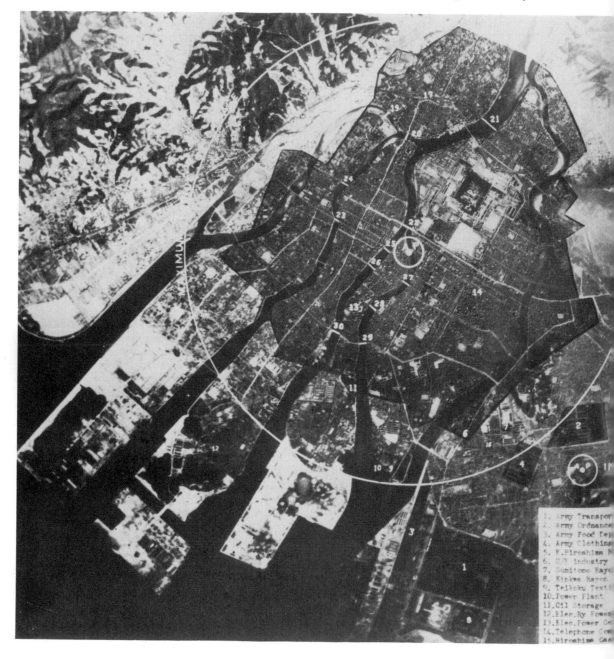

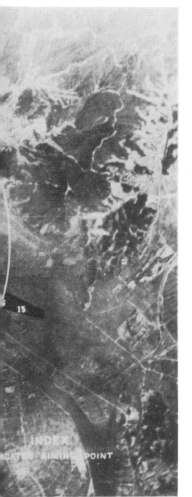

A reconnaissance picture of Hiroshima indicates the exact spot where Ferebee was to drop the atom bomb.

pills, one for each man – just in case the plane was shot down over Japan after completing its mission.

As the *Enola Gay* made its climb, Japanese radar had already picked it up and was monitoring the course of all three planes as they headed towards Hiroshima. Earlier, at 7.09 a.m., their radar had detected the weather plane, *Straight Flush*. An air-raid warning had been given in Hiroshima as the plane flew overhead.

At 7.24 a.m. Tibbets picked up a radio message from Eatherley in *Straight Flush*: "Cloud cover less than three tenths, all altitudes. Advice: bomb primary." Tibbets relayed the news to his crew over the intercom: "It's Hiroshima."

At about 8.05 Van Kirk, the navigator, announced: "Ten minutes to AP." AP was the airforce abbreviation for aiming point. At an earlier briefing session Thomas Ferebee, the bombardier, had studied aerial photographs of Hiroshima and had noticed an unusual T-shaped bridge joining three islands in the centre of the city. The Aioi Bridge was one of Hiroshima's most distinctive landmarks and it was to be Ferebee's aiming point.

The minutes ticked away as the bomber closed in on its target. In Hiroshima, thirty miles to the north-west, warning of an air-raid had been given and then cancelled. Japanese radar had lost track of the *Enola Gay* and its two escort planes. At 8.12 a.m. Van Kirk signalled the start of the bombing run. Ferebee crouched over his bomb sights.

The skies were blue and clear and, from an altitude of 9,460 metres, Ferebee could see the city spreading out over the delta beneath him like a vast map. The observation planes circled above, as the *Enola Gay* came on remorselessly.

From his cockpit, Paul Tibbets called out over the intercom: "On glasses!" All crewmen except the pilot and bombardier pulled their special issue black, polarized goggles over their eyes.

Ferebee now had the Aioi Bridge in his sights. "I've got it," he said, and threw a switch that gave every one of the bomber's crewmen a synchronized bleep, second by second, over their earphones. When the bleeps stopped, "Little Boy" would have left the plane. The bleeps ceased at precisely 08:15:17.

At the moment Ferebee yelled: "Bomb away!", Tibbets threw the plane into a violent right-hand turn towards the sea. The crewmen caught their breath and held on.

Forty-three seconds after the bomb had left the plane, a sudden flare lit up the faces of the *Enola Gay*'s crew.

Ground zero: 8.16 a.m.

In Hiroshima city centre the streets were crowded with people on their way to work. Shops and banks were opening. Queues began to form as word got round that certain items were now on sale in this shop or in that department store. Two crowded trams passed one another on the Aioi Bridge. People on bicycles weaved between the passing trams.

High up in the clear sky hung four clear vapour trails. The *Enola Gay* could be seen as a tiny dot far above the city.

*   *   *   *   *   *   *

The T-shaped Aioi Bridge was squarely in the centre of Major Thomas Ferebee's bomb sights. He squeezed the button, releasing the atom bomb. The *Enola Gay* rose suddenly as nearly 4½ tonnes weight was released. Moments later, Tibbets put the *Enola Gay* into a steep dive, banking the heavy plane seawards as he did so.

*   *   *   *   *   *   *

The unearthly howl of the diving bomber could be heard clearly at ground level, even though the plane was nearly 6 miles above. It made the people stop and look up. A parachute opened and a tiny dot floated slowly down towards the city centre. Suddenly there was a gigantic, blinding flash . . . .

In one instant more than 4½ square miles of the city was flattened; tens of thousands of people died. Fires raged, smoke, debris and dust rose into the air. In all the world there had never been a man-made explosion on this scale before. It was as if the most violent forces of nature had come together in one huge and devastating volcanic eruption.

"Little Boy" had been fused to explode at 564 metres above ground level, for maximum destructive effect. At the centre of the explosion, a fireball of nuclear energy burned for a moment as hot as the surface of the sun. Heat inside the fireball was calculated to have reached 299,982°C, while at "ground zero", the centre of the explosion at ground level, temperatures must have been at least 6,093°C. At this heat, roof tiles melted, granite building slabs bubbled and human beings simply vapourized. All wooden buildings within two miles of "ground zero" spontaneously burst into flames.

However, the heat generated by the nuclear explosion

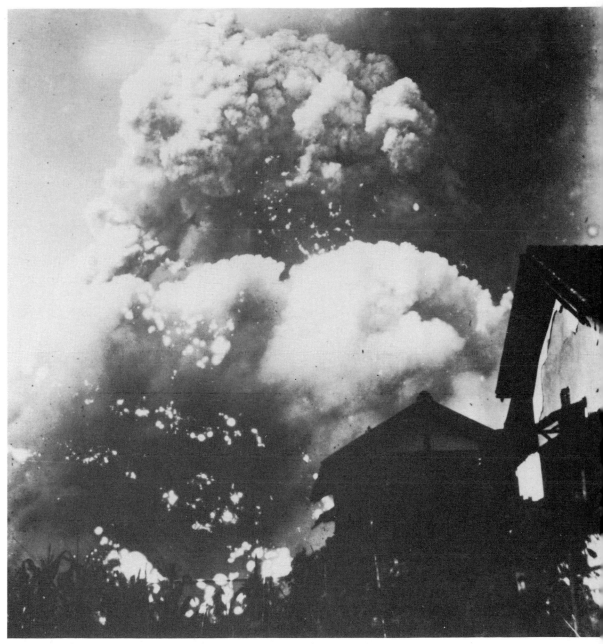

Two minutes after the explosion a fireball engulfs Hiroshima. Dust, dirt and debris rise into the air to form the mushroom cloud.

accounted for only a third of the total energy released. At least a half of the bomb's destructive effect came from its explosive blast, and the remaining energy was in the form of radioactivity. At the centre of the explosion (the epicentre) air pressure reached 8 tonnes per square metre. The compressed and heated air became visible, like a grey wall, as

it rushed outwards in every direction, at a rate of 400 metres per second.

While most people near ground zero were vapourized, some survived the heat and the blast, sheltered by concrete buildings. These survivors all bore witness to one main point: that there was a gigantic flash and then silence. No noise was heard or remembered. Further away, the noise of the explosion was deafening.

These people also told some strange and horrific stories of their experiences near "ground zero". One man swore he saw the Aioi Bridge rise several metres in the air before coming down to rest on its foundations. Another remembered standing on the pavement outside a tall building. There was a blinding flash and he lost consciousness. On waking up moments later, he found himself on a ledge of the building three floors up. The blast from the bomb had literally swept him into the air like a feather. Incredibly, the man was unhurt! Eyewitnesses also saw the waters of the Ohta river rise up into the air like a giant waterspout.

*   *   *   *   *   *   *

Industrial Promotion Hall 日軍業獎勵館　Motoyasu River 元安川　Honkawa River 本川　Honkawa Primary School 本川小学校　Aioi Bridge (T. Bridge) 相生橋 (丁字橋)　Koi 己斐町

(Left) *Devastation after the dropping of the atom bomb on Hiroshima. The concrete buildings that survived were built to withstand earthquakes. The panoramic view (above) was taken from near ground zero, one month after the explosion.*

Miles from its target, the *Enola Gay* and its two escort planes had succeeded in slipping beyond the grasp of the tremendous explosion. Inside the *Enola Gay* crew members wearing dark polarized goggles shielded their eyes as the bomb's detonation released an intense glare of energy many times brighter than the sun. From the centre of the explosion a grey dome of compressed air rushed outwards. There was no noise, no sound of any sort. Seconds later it hit them: a powerful shock wave, the sound of the exploding bomb, caught the plane and tossed it about like a child's toy.

Tibbets thought the plane had been hit by anti-aircraft fire. "Flak!" he yelled over his intercom. Then he heard the rumble of the explosion like a clap of thunder and knew the plane had simply caught the tail end of the atom bomb's blast. Another shock wave hit the plane.

Then a column of fire, smoke and dust rose above the city. The fiery column began mushrooming out at a height of about 2,500 metres. One minute after the bomb exploded, the mushroom cloud reached a height of 7,000 metres and was rising fast.

Lieutenant Caron had the best view of the explosion. As he spoke over the plane's intercom system, his words were tape-recorded:

"A column of smoke rising fast. It has a fiery red core. A bubbling mass, purple grey in colour, with that red core. It's all turbulent. Fires are springing up everywhere, like flames shooting out of a huge bed of coals . . . . Here

21

The mushroom cloud rises over the stricken city.

it comes, the mushroom shape . . . . It's like a mass of bubbling molasses . . . it's nearly level with me and climbing . . . ."

By now the mushroom cloud, reaching 10,000 metres into the earth's atmosphere, hung like a gigantic gravestone over Hiroshima. What had been a bustling city of 245,000 people was now a smoking ruin. Tibbets radioed the successful completion of the mission to his base. News would quickly reach the US President.

*   *   *   *   *   *   *

Satoshi Nakamura, a reporter for the Domei News Agency, was taking breakfast in his house eight miles west of Hiroshima. When the bomb exploded he couldn't believe his eyes. At the time he thought an ammunition factory had blown up. Such a massive explosion could not have been caused by a single bomb. But had the entire city been destroyed? It could not be possible.

Satoshi needed information. He picked up his telephone but it was dead. The lines that connected him to the outside world all passed through Hiroshima. There was nothing he could do but see the extent of the damage for himself. Satoshi got into his car and headed for the rising column of smoke . . . .

The bomb caught Tatsuko Mori and her father-in-law on open ground near a reservoir on the outskirts of the city. Tatsuko, carrying her child on her back, had directed the old man's gaze to the tiny parachute floating above the city. She sensed something was wrong. When the bomb exploded, everything seemed unreal. Tatsuko remembered being enveloped by what seemed like a huge magnesium flare. Dragging the old man with her, she instinctively rushed for cover between two nearby houses. The air was full of flying glass.

Taking the child from her back, Tatsuko found his tiny body covered in blood. Slowly and carefully she picked out the long pieces of splintered glass where they stuck into his flesh. There was a rumble like thunder overhead. The entire city was ablaze . . . .

Susumu Kimura described the moment when the bomb exploded as like seeing fireworks. She was inside the house with her mother. She remembered an intense light which flashed from red to yellow. Outside, the surrounding houses disintegrated, windows were blown in, walls collapsed and roofs were lifted off with the force of the blast.

Susumu was blown to the floor. When she came to her senses, she was in the open. Her mother was holding her and weeping gently. Through the swirling smoke and dust, Susumu could see ghostly forms of people wandering around as if in a trance. Some of them were clothed; most were not. The heat and the blast had burned the clothes from their bodies. Thin strips of what looked like cloth hung from the bodies of these people. Then Susumu realized that the trailing material was not cloth at all, but human skin . . . .

The sights that greeted Satoshi Nakamura when he arrived in Hiroshima were horrific beyond belief. On the outskirts of the city people were lying by the roadside. Most of the skin had been burnt from their bodies. Many cried out for water, but if anyone were to give water to any of these burns victims they would die; without skin, their bodies were simply too fragile to take in either food or water. There was no medical aid.

Fires everywhere. Some people lay trapped beneath the wreckage of their homes. They were burned to death. Towards the centre, the city was entirely flattened. Only the shattered reinforced-concrete shells of a few buildings

Air-raid shelters in Hiroshima were typically partly below ground, with timber frames and covered with earth. Whilst they provided some protection against high-explosive bombs, they became a death-trap in a fire-storm.

Just a few hours after the blast, dazed survivors gather at a first aid station.

remained. Satoshi recognized the steel framework of a dome and the shattered concrete facade of what had once been the imposing Shorei-kan, Hiroshima's Industry Promotion Building. Across the city the earth was scorched to a strange reddish-brown colour.

Near Hiroshima station, a packed commuter train was now a twisted metal skeleton. Inside the carriages, blackened corpses occupied the seats or stood still clutching the leather straps that hung from the ceiling.

The walls of shattered buildings had further stories to tell. In some places you could plainly see the shadows of people as they had been standing when the atom bomb exploded. The huge flash and the thermal radiation had actually created "photographic" imprints of anything that had cast a shadow.

The shadow of a ladder burned onto the surface of a storage tank. The black tar that was shaded absorbed the heat, but the area directly exposed to thermal radiation melted.

Shigem Orimen, a middle-school student, was beside the Honkawa River, near the centre of the explosion, to do demolition work as part of student mobilization. He had set down his lunch box when the explosion occurred. The lunch in his box turned to charcoal. The entire class of 343 first-year students died.

Death was on every side. Countless bloated corpses floated on the Ohta river.

Two hours after the bomb dropped, a strange black rain began to fall on Hiroshima as it burned. Black drops as big as the ends of one's fingers rained steadily on to the ruins, damping down fires. Satoshi noticed that the strange rain drops left a black, greasy stain on his clothing that would not wash off.

In his journey around the outskirts of the city, Satoshi hunted among the damaged buildings for a telephone that still worked. It was urgent that outside help be sent at once. Already soldiers and medical teams from outlying areas were beginning to arrive, but there was no one to co-ordinate the aid that was so badly needed. By midday Satoshi had found what he was looking for. In the offices of the Japan Broadcasting Corporation, three miles from "ground zero", was a working telephone.

Satoshi called the regional office of his news agency, asking that his report be relayed at once to Tokyo. Over the line, he read his news story slowly and deliberately. "At around 8.16 a.m., August 6th, one or two enemy planes flew over Hiroshima and dropped one or two special bombs . . .

completely destroying the city. Casualties are estimated to be 170,000 dead."

Later that afternoon, Satoshi rang the agency again to give a more detailed account. He asked whether the shocking news he had reported was now in the newspapers. He was told that it was not. The agency's news editor quite simply did not believe Satoshi's story. No bomb on earth could have killed 170,000 people and destroyed an entire city.

Tatsuko Mori took her injured child and made her way to her parents-in-law's home outside the city. Her father-in-law accompanied her. When she had reached safety she found her mother-in-law waiting for her. Tatsuko never saw her husband again.

Susumu Kimura's father had survived the bomb and made his way back home to find his wife and younger daughter safe. Together the family made their way among the ruins in search of Susumu's sister. On the sides of ruined buildings people had scrawled messages asking for information about missing

Dr Kaoru Shima was out of town when the bomb fell. He rushed back to Hiroshima and put a board at the spot where his hospital used to stand, asking for information about patients and staff.

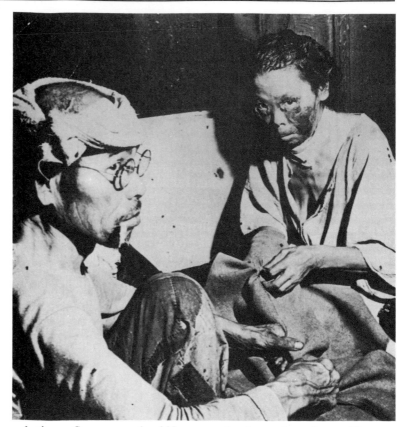

Many survivors suffered horrific burns.

relatives. Susumu asked if anyone had seen her sister. No one had.

* * * * * * *

In the United States, during the morning of 6th August, the scientists whose hard work had made the atom bomb possible were waiting for news of the *Enola Gay*'s mission. They were all part of a top-secret team based at the Los Alamos research centre, deep in the remote Pecos Mountains of New Mexico. For the centre's forty-year-old director, J. Robert Oppenheimer, two years of working under constant and intense pressure were at an end. In those years, he had built up a team of scientists from all over the world and his energy and determination had kept them going. Just three weeks earlier they had put their ideas to the test: a plutonium bomb, "Fat Man", had been successfully detonated at a desert site near Alamogordo in southern New Mexico. The work had taken its toll on "Oppy", as his colleagues affectionately called him. He was now frail and gaunt – a chain smoker. His weight had fallen to just 7½ stone.

At around 9.30 a.m. (local time) a message was received by radio from Captain Parsons in the *Enola Gay*: fifteen minutes earlier the atom bomb code-named "Little Boy" had exploded above the city of Hiroshima, destroying everything within a two-mile radius.

Oppenheimer was jubilant. Immediately he called together the centre's entire research staff in one of the camp's lecture theatres. Amid cheers and shouts he strode to the speaker's platform, clasping his hands above his head in a gesture of triumph. 6th August was Oppenheimer's day of celebration. The important role he had played in the race to develop the atom bomb would be acknowledged publicly. For a brief while he would be a national hero.

*   *   *   *   *   *   *

At 2.58 p.m. the *Enola Gay*, its mission completed, landed back on Tinian. The purpose of the mission and its success had been announced, and the entire base had been assembled to meet the bomber and its escort of observation planes. A military band played and General Spaatz and his second in command, General Curtis Le May, drove up in a jeep to where the *Enola Gay* had halted on the runway. As Tibbets climbed down from the aircraft, Spaatz stepped forward and pinned the Distinguished Service Cross on his flying suit. Cameras clicked.

Paul Tibbets is given the Distinguished Service Cross.

THE INVESTIGATION

How did science and technology enable the first atom bomb to be built?

Splitting the atom

Albert Einstein. The atomic bomb was dramatic proof of his Theory of Relativity.

In 1905 Albert Einstein published his famous Theory of Relativity defining the nature of the universe. Einstein observed that space and time were not constant at all but were relative to the speed of light. He explained that all matter that existed in the universe contained an enormous amount of energy. That energy was "locked up" inside the atom.

Einstein's theories were expressed in the equation, $E = MC^2$: energy (E) was equal to the mass of an object (M) multiplied by the square of the speed of light (C^2). At the time of Einstein's theory it was widely believed that the atom – the building-block of all matter – could not be split into smaller particles. If atoms could be split, then the locked-up energy of which Einstein spoke would be released.

When Einstein published his Theory, little was known about the exact nature of the atom. Experiments to discover more focused on an element called radium. Discovered by Marie Curie in 1898, radium was found to give off tiny electrically charged particles even smaller than atoms. These came from within broken atoms. The energy given off by the radium was called radioactivity.

In Britain in 1919, Ernest Rutherford discovered that the particles emitted by radium were able to split atoms of nitrogen, altering those atoms in the process to form oxygen. Atom research gathered speed. Two types of electrically charged particles were discovered – positive (protons) and negative (electrons). The positive and negative particles created an electrical force that held the structure of the atom together. Since positive and negative repelled one another, particles from one atom could not break free and enter another atom unless something occurred to upset their natural balance. In radium this natural balance did not exist.

Positive and negative particles were unevenly matched and the loosely formed atoms were thus able to disintegrate. But how were radium's protons and electrons able to penetrate the atoms of other elements without being repelled? Scientists looked for the answer.

In 1932 came an important new discovery. A British scientist, James Chadwick, identified a third type of particle within the atom, that had no electric charge. He called it the neutron. It was this particle that was able to split atoms.

Nuclear energy At this stage, research into atom splitting (nuclear fission) was regarded as a purely scientific concern, of little interest outside academic circles. But this view was overturned when in 1939 two German scientists, Otto Hahn and Fritz Strassman, discovered that if a substance called uranium was bombarded with neutrons it would set up an independent nuclear chain reaction. Once split, a uranium atom released neutrons which, in turn, split other atoms. This process would continue repeating itself, releasing radioactive energy at an ever-increasing rate.

When the chain reaction had accelerated to a certain level, the uranium was said to have reached critical mass and at this

Nuclear fission.

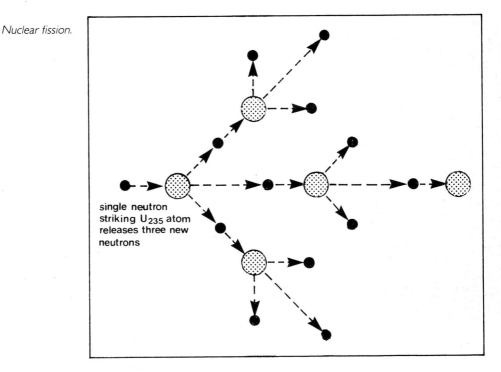

single neutron striking U_{235} atom releases three new neutrons

point the fast-splitting atoms would cause an uncontrollable explosion of energy. However, critical mass could be avoided by slowing down the neutrons and hence the rate at which the uranium atoms were split. Various elements such as carbon and boron were found to absorb neutrons safely. Bringing a carbon rod into contact with the uranium would slow down the chain reaction and keep it at a safe level. In this case the energy released by the nuclear chain reaction could be harnessed to provide electricity.

Hahn and Strassman's experiments had been carried out with a tiny amount of unrefined uranium ore. Nevertheless, the possibilities of nuclear fission had been demonstrated.

The race for nuclear weapons begins

The German scientists realized how important their findings would be for the rest of the world and in June 1939 they published a paper announcing their discovery to scientists in other countries. It seems incredible that Germany's Nazi leaders allowed two of their foremost scientists to publish sensitive research papers only months before the outbreak of the Second World War.

In more peaceful times, Hahn and Strassman's discovery might have been greeted as the dawning of a new age of cheap and abundant energy. Knowledge would be shared and humankind would reap the benefits of industrial growth and prosperity. With Europe on the brink of war, however, scientists and politicians were quick to realize that nuclear energy was many times more powerful and destructive than conventional high explosives. A race to develop a nuclear bomb began. The USA, Britain, France and Russia all sponsored nuclear research. Japan also had her own group of physicists working on a nuclear project. But formidable problems lay before these various research teams.

Weapons research gets under way

Obtaining sufficient uranium ore for experiments and for the eventual manufacture of a bomb was a major problem. The only known sources of the metal were in Canada, Czechoslovakia and the Belgian Congo. Scientists had yet to perfect a method of refining uranium in sufficient quantities to make a bomb. Nothing was known about how much uranium would be needed or what the explosive effects of the bomb might be. In these early days it was thought that several tonnes of uranium might be needed to set off a nuclear explosion. US scientists first estimated that the force of such an explosion could be the equivalent of anything from 500 to 1,500 tonnes of TNT. So governments were at first cautious about investing the vast sums of money necessary for further research in this area. The high costs forced Russia, Japan and France to abandon their efforts, but research continued in the USA, Britain and Germany.

In spite of the need for enormous amounts of government money to finance nuclear research, everything finally depended on the skill and dedication of the scientists working on the project. Many of the top scientists in Britain and the USA were Jewish and had fled from Nazi Germany to escape persecution. The intensity of their efforts to develop an atom bomb was born of their fear of Nazism and of the consequences for the world if Germany succeeded in becoming a nuclear power.

Research in Britain and the United States

In March 1940, John Dunning, a scientist at Columbia University in the USA, identified a particular type of uranium atom (U235) that was much easier to split than other atoms of the metal. U235 atoms could be split by the neutrons naturally present in radioactive uranium. If uranium could be refined to contain only U235 atoms, then an explosive chain reaction would be more likely to occur. Because that chain reaction would be faster than that possible with ordinary uranium, a smaller amount of U235 would be needed to create an explosion.

Since only one in every one hundred uranium atoms was of the 235 variety, vast quantities of ore would have to be broken down and refined to obtain the small amount needed to produce a nuclear bomb. With atomic research still in its infancy there was much debate about the most effective ways of separating uranium atoms for industry. What might work in a laboratory might be unsafe or impractical on a large scale.

The practicalities of extracting U235 from refined uranium were investigated by two Jewish scientists who had fled to Britain from Nazi Germany. Otto Frisch and Rudolf Peierls not only calculated the amount of U235 needed to cause a nuclear explosion but also suggested ways in which the U235 could be extracted in sufficient quantities to make a bomb. Their method was to turn the uranium into a gas and then separate the uranium atoms according to their weight. U235 atoms were recognizably heavier than their counterparts.

In 1941 plutonium – a by-product of nuclear fission – was discovered independently in both Britain and the United States. This new, artificially created element was found to be more likely to undergo a nuclear chain reaction than U235. Even less plutonium would therefore be needed to make a bomb and, given the enormous time that it took to extract even minute quantities of U235, this was considered a major breakthrough in the bid to build a bomb before the Germans. While Uranium 235 was to be used to make the Hiroshima bomb, plutonium formed the core of the second atom bomb which was dropped on Nagasaki.

The B29 story The development of the B29 bomber, the plane that was to drop the first atom bomb, was an almost parallel technical achievement to the development of the bomb itself. At the outbreak of the Second World War, the United States government foresaw that if Britain fell, Germany would be a potential enemy on the other side of the Atlantic. The US needed a plane capable of bombing targets in Europe. Such a super-bomber would act as a deterrent to Nazi aggression.

The new bomber needed to be capable of flying at altitudes never before reached by aircraft, both to conserve fuel and to avoid anti-aircraft fire. Designers overcame the problems of high-altitude flying with the revolutionary concept of pressurized cabins. Inside these specially strengthened compartments air could be kept at the same pressure as at ground level. Thus there was no need for the bomber's crew to wear oxygen masks or extra-warm clothing to protect them against the sub-zero temperatures at high altitude.

The Boeing Aircraft Corporation submitted a design which was approved by the US government almost a year before the USA finally went to war. Boeing's new bomber, the B29, was so complex that many different aircraft companies and components industries were needed to manufacture all its parts. The building of the B29 called for industrial co-operation on a scale never previously experienced. By the time the USA was at war, her aircraft and armaments industries had been fully mobilized.

The first B29 was test-flown in September 1942 and the first production-line aircraft were available in April of the following year. Too late to see effective service in Europe, the B29 was the one aircraft capable of bombing Japan from bases in India and China and from the remote Pacific islands that eventually fell to US forces.

Why did Britain and the USA decide to make the bomb?

A letter to President Roosevelt

In the United States, the news of Hahn and Strassman's discovery of the nuclear chain reaction worried one man in particular. Leo Szilard, a Jewish scientist, had emigrated to America from Hungary to avoid Nazi persecution. Szilard reasoned that if the German government had allowed this scientific discovery to be published, then it must know a great deal more than it chose to reveal. Perhaps German scientists were on the verge of a major breakthrough in atom research and had authorized the publication of Hahn and Strassman's experiments as a warning to the rest of the world.

One further factor worried Szilard: that Germany had banned all exports of uranium from the Nazi-controlled mines in Czechoslovakia. Szilard lost no time in trying to alert the United States government to the German threat. He contacted the world's most famous physicist, Albert Einstein, who at that time was living in the United States. Together they decided to write a letter to President Franklin D. Roosevelt, in which they explained the full implications of Hahn and Strassman's findings and asked for an immediate research programme to be set up that would enable the United States to develop her own atom bomb. If enough financial resources could be found, there was a chance that America might beat the Germans in the race to build the new weapon and thereby assure her own survival.

On 11th October, 1939, the letter was delivered personally to the President by Einstein's friend, Alexander Sachs. Sachs was a senior government economist who had worked closely with Roosevelt and was trusted by him.

Roosevelt backs nuclear research

The direct approach convinced Roosevelt of the need for the USA to begin her own nuclear research programme. However, America was not at war, and so it was with caution that Roosevelt set up a committee to coordinate and direct the research. At first, this committee did no more than encourage the independent research that was taking place in universities all over the USA, particularly at Berkeley, Columbia and Chicago.

Britain and the bomb

From the early 1930s Britain had been one of the leading nations in the field of nuclear research. Following Hahn and Strassman's discoveries scientists were urged by the government to devote their efforts to weapons research. The war against Germany gave the British government a sense of urgency and of purpose even greater than that of the United States.

At first, British scientists cooperated freely, though unofficially, with their American counterparts. The USA was actively helping Britain's war effort by supplying arms and making available her latest military technology. In March 1941 the US Senate passed the Lend-Lease Act enabling Britain to borrow warships and place unlimited orders for armaments in exchange for long leases on certain British naval and military bases overseas. The Lend-Lease Act defined Britain's defence as "vital to US interests".

But American help on the nuclear front was inadequate. By the middle of 1941, British research was so far advanced that Britain's Prime Minister, Winston Churchill, actually considered pressing on with the development of the atom bomb without US assistance. On 27th August, 1941, Churchill received a confidential memo from his scientific adviser, Lord Cherwell. Cherwell claimed that scientists working on a British nuclear bomb were confident that "the odds are ten to one on success within two years". On the subject of building plants to refine uranium, Cherwell warned that "However much I may trust my neighbour and depend on him, I am very much averse to putting myself completely at his mercy. I would therefore not press the Americans to undertake this work . . . ."

Cherwell's memo evidently influenced Churchill's policy making for on 3rd September he announced to his chiefs of staff that no expense would be spared in building a uranium bomb as soon as possible. A plant was actually built in North Wales to separate Uranium 235. A similar plant was planned in Canada, which was at that time a British dominion. That same month Churchill turned down an offer by Roosevelt that their two countries should work together to develop an atom bomb.

The Manhattan Project On 7th December, 1941, Japanese light bombers launched from aircraft carriers attacked the US Pacific fleet anchored at its base at Pearl Harbor in the Hawaiian Islands. In this surprise attack the bulk of the Pacific fleet was sunk or put out of action. On 8th December Britain and the United States declared war on Japan and on 11th December Germany and Italy, Japan's allies, declared war on the United States.

President Roosevelt now needed no persuasion to give top

priority to the development of nuclear weapons. Before the end of the year a joint military and civilian project was set up with access to almost unlimited funds. Thus the Manhattan Project was born – named after the headquarters of its first military director in the Manhattan district of New York.

Britain, meanwhile, began to realize that the development of a nuclear bomb was going to be very costly. Churchill's scientific committee estimated costs to be in the region of £8,500,000. This was almost certainly a serious underestimate considering the eventual cost of the American research programme, which was over fifty times that.

As the Manhattan Project gathered momentum, so British research lagged behind. The only possible way for Britain to obtain nuclear weapons was to cease independent research and become partners with the Americans. Whereas in September 1941 Churchill had turned down Roosevelt's offer to develop a bomb in partnership, now he had to agree to almost any terms in order to share the benefits of the atom bomb when it was eventually ready for use against the common enemy. The terms that Churchill agreed to were laid down in the Treaty of Quebec, signed in Canada on 19th August, 1943.

The Quebec Agreement, known to few people besides the two heads of state and their personal advisers, was to remain a secret for fifteen years. Both sides agreed that the bomb should be used only by joint consent and that no information about the bomb or its development should be given to any other country – even an ally, such as the Soviet Union. Britain was to send her nuclear scientists to join the Manhattan Project, now established at Los Alamos, for the duration of the war.

Roosevelt died suddenly on 12th April, 1945, and was replaced by his Vice President, Harry S. Truman. Truman, though doubtless aware of the Quebec Agreement, ignored it totally. In the immediate aftermath of World War II, Britain was excluded from any participation in American nuclear technology and had to develop her own atom bomb in secret. Co-operation between Britain and America returned only after Britain had built and tested her own hydrogen bomb at Christmas Island in 1958.

The Nazis' nuclear programme In December 1944 American and British troops closing in on Germany found the research centre where work on a German atom bomb was thought to have been taking place. Scientists taken prisoner revealed that, starved of funds, their own project had made little progress. Some of the German scientists, too, had had moral objections to the research they had been asked to carry out. They had deliberately created difficulties to slow down their team's research work.

The suspected German atom bomb that had spurred on the British and Americans in their research was therefore of no real danger. Now that the Allies' fears had been proved groundless, many of the scientists working on the Manhattan Project wanted to abandon their research. But, by that stage, their own bomb was nearing completion and their political masters were anxious to see it ready for use against Japan.

How was the atom bomb developed?

Early in 1942 James C. Marshall of the Army Corps of Engineers was put in charge of the joint military and civilian nuclear research programme. His offices in the Manhattan district of New York gave the name "Manhattan Project" to the work being carried out at universities up and down the USA. But Marshall was so obsessed by army red tape that orders for vital equipment were often held up while the "correct" paperwork was completed.

On 16th September, 1942, he was replaced by General Leslie R. Groves, a much more forceful and aggressive character who viewed his scientists with a mixture of amused tolerance and suspicion. Groves realized quickly that effective administration was not the only key to success. He needed to appoint a civilian director who would be able to understand, motivate and encourage the project's highly individualistic team of scientists. In Julius Robert Oppenheimer, a young physicist, Groves saw all the qualities of leadership that he desired.

Oppenheimer and Groves

By the end of 1942 Groves had decided to bring all the scientists together in one place. You could not coordinate or control work being carried out in different research centres. From the first, Groves took Oppenheimer into his confidence. Oppenheimer helped Groves set up his new laboratories and order all the equipment needed. He also helped to organize different research departments in the fields of theoretical and experimental physics, chemistry, metallurgy and weapon design.

◁ *Alamogordo: Oppenheimer and Groves inspect the remains of the steel tower on which the first atom bomb was exploded.*

So as to attract as little attention as possible, the site for the new research establishment needed to be remote. Oppenheimer and his wife Kitty owned a ranch in the Pecos Mountains of New Mexico, where they would retreat for quiet weekends when Robert was not teaching at the California State University at Berkeley. Near the Oppenheimers' ranch was a small boys' school, Los Alamos.

Oppenheimer took Groves to visit the school. The two men agreed that it would make an ideal location for the research centre that Groves wanted to build. Occupying part of a large raised plateau or *mesa*, Los Alamos could be reached only by means of a winding and bumpy road. The nearest town of any size was the tiny city of Santa Fé, some forty miles to the south-east. Not only was Los Alamos a long way from built-up areas, it could also be easily guarded against intruders – the steep sides of the *mesa* were difficult to climb.

Within weeks of Groves' visit, Los Alamos was requisitioned by the US government and construction teams moved in. Oppenheimer was appointed the civilian director of the new establishment in February 1943 and on 15th April Los Alamos began its new life as a nuclear research centre.

A city of scientists

The immense difficulties of setting up the centre were overcome largely thanks to Oppenheimer. First there was the problem of persuading civilian scientists to leave their homes and live in a remote colony cut off from the outside world. To preserve secrecy, Groves had decreed that the staff of Los Alamos should not be allowed to receive visitors. Furthermore, the scientists were seldom allowed to leave the confines of their colony. All the basic amenities of life would be provided within the camp itself.

To attract staff to the Manhattan Project, Oppenheimer cleverly used as bait the names of a few top scientists who had already joined. Working for the Project was presented as an opportunity to participate in one of the greatest scientific challenges of the twentieth century. It was also an opportunity for people to contribute to the overthrow of Nazi Germany and her allies.

Married men or women were allowed to bring their families but single people had to come alone. In a very short space of time, it became clear that by far the most pressing problem for

Los Alamos: a shanty town of wooden huts.

Oppenheimer was the provision of amenities for the growing colony of scientists and their families.

Housing consisted merely of prefabricated huts, each of which had to accommodate several families. Each family was usually limited to two rooms with a shared bathroom and toilet. Piped water supplies were drawn from a local spring and a drainage and sewage system was constructed.

Shops, a school, a post office and a laundry were all made ready as the first families moved in. A camp hospital quickly followed, but less basic needs such as entertainment took longer to satisfy.

At the outset, Los Alamos contained 254 army personnel and over twice as many civilians. By 1945 the colony had been expanded to accommodate 2,000 soldiers and around 4,000 civilians. But the dramatic increase in the camp's population was not due entirely to Oppenheimer's recruitment drive. The colony had an important effect on family life that Oppenheimer had not anticipated. There was so little for the young married scientists to do in the evening that the birth rate shot up alarmingly!

Eventually the lack of entertainment at Los Alamos was remedied and the camp came to boast a nineteen-piece band, a choir, an orchestra and its own radio station, as well as a cinema and a beer hall.

Under the army's
watchful eye
The large army garrison stationed at Los Alamos did not interfere with the work of the civilian scientists, technicians and office staff. Their function was to act as administrators to the Project and to ensure tight security. All letters to and from individuals working at Los Alamos had to be routed through an anonymous post office box number in Santa Fé. All mail was read by army censors and individuals were subject to security checks to investigate their past political views. When military police uncovered the previous communist affiliations of his wife and brother, Oppenheimer himself was suspected of being a "security risk". Despite the fact that General Groves himself dismissed this evidence as irrelevant, the communist connection was to be re-examined during the post-war "witch hunts" of Senator James MacCarthy.

While Oppenheimer's own loyalty was beyond question, two scientists were later discovered to have passed vital information on to Soviet agents. The Soviet Union's rapid progress in developing her own atom bomb following the success of the Manhattan Project was no doubt due in part to this security leak.

Uranium and plutonium production

Besides Los Alamos, General Groves also oversaw the vast civil engineering projects to build the production plants for extracting and refining uranium and its derivative, plutonium. Once built, the plants were operated by the large private chemical company, Du Pont.

Two of these plants, sited at Oak Ridge, Tennessee, employed 13,000 people. One of the plants used a vast electro-magnetic device called a calutron to separate U235 atoms. The calutron's electro-magnet was so huge that there was simply not enough copper available in the United States to make the wire needed for its high-conductivity windings. A reluctant US Treasury was persuaded to lend the Project 6,000 tonnes of silver bullion with which to do the job.

Besides the refining plants at Oak Ridge, a brand-new city had to be built near the site to house the plants' workers and their families. Not one of these people knew the exact purpose of the work they were carrying out. This was to remain a secret until the news of the Hiroshima bomb was announced and the war with Japan was practically over.

Oak Ridge Works, Tennessee. This plant, started from scratch as part of the Manhattan Project, employed 13,000 people who worked to produce uranium 235 for the core of the Hiroshima bomb.

At Hanford in Washington State, an atomic pile, or what is now called a nuclear reactor, generated power through a controlled chain reaction and produced plutonium as a by-product. Hanford took a construction team of 45,000 men more than a year to build.

It is easy to see why the development costs of the first atom bomb came to more than two thousand million dollars.

"Little Boy" and
"Fat Man"

The development of the atom bomb at Los Alamos is a rather complicated story. In fact, not one but three different types of bomb were designed. Of these, two – "Little Boy" and "Fat Man" – were used against Japan. A third – the hydrogen bomb – was immensely more powerful but was not ready until 1952.

The reason for spreading the research over several types of bomb was uncertainty about the supply of the fissionable raw materials, uranium and plutonium. Groves had authorized the building of massive plants to refine these materials but no one could foresee which one might be delivered by the deadline given, or whether it would then be available in sufficient quantity.

The uranium "Little Boy" bomb was the simplest in terms of design. A plug of uranium would be fired into a hollow cylinder of the same substance, thereby assembling enough fissionable material to reach critical mass – the point at which a nuclear chain reaction would cause the uranium to explode. 100 kg of refined U235 was needed to make just one bomb.

Far less plutonium – only 2 kg – was needed to produce a similar explosion. But plutonium was a far more difficult substance to handle. The "Fat Man" bomb was therefore designed as a series of spheres within spheres. At the very centre was a polonium core, the source of neutrons needed to start an explosive chain reaction. Surrounding that was a sphere of highly fissionable plutonium, the size of a grapefruit; and a larger sphere of uranium prevented the plutonium sphere from losing neutrons. Separated, these spheres were harmless. But surrounding "Fat Man's" radioactive spheres was an outer steel casing made up of a series of explosive "lenses" designed to direct their force inwards, not outwards. When the explosive lenses were detonated they would cause the bomb's radioactive spheres to implode, or be compressed into one another, setting off an instantaneous explosive chain reaction.

The bombs are
tested

By late spring 1945, work on the uranium and plutonium bombs was nearing completion. Full-sized mock-ups of both bombs had been made, and test drops from aircraft had provided valuable feedback on flight stability and the operation of the radar-controlled fuse that would detonate the bomb at a predetermined height.

Sizable quantities of refined uranium and plutonium now began to arrive at Los Alamos from the Oak Ridge and Hanford plants and, on 18th June, a party of scientists and

Little Boy and Fat Man. The photographs were released to the press only in 1960.

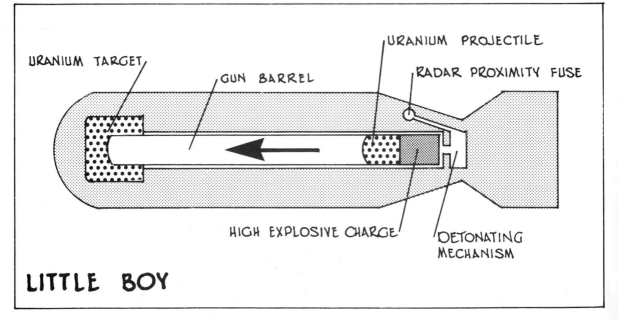

URANIUM TARGET

URANIUM PROJECTILE

RADAR PROXIMITY FUSE

GUN BARREL

HIGH EXPLOSIVE CHARGE

DETONATING MECHANISM

LITTLE BOY

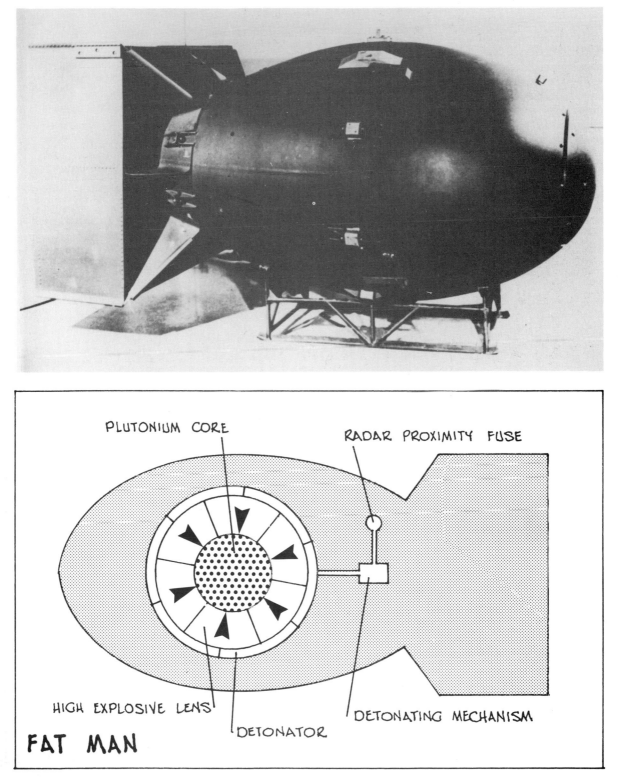

PLUTONIUM CORE

RADAR PROXIMITY FUSE

HIGH EXPLOSIVE LENS

DETONATOR

DETONATING MECHANISM

FAT MAN

technicians left Los Alamos for the tiny Pacific island air base of Tinian, where work began on assembling the two atom bombs.

But before an atom bomb could be dropped, Los Alamos was asked to stage a test firing. The explosion and its after-effects would be carefully documented on film and measured by scientific instruments. A desert site in the middle of an airforce bombing range at Alamogordo, New Mexico, was chosen for the test. A "Fat Man" plutonium bomb was winched to the top of a steel tower especially erected in the middle of the desert. Oppenheimer and his team made their final preparations.

Just before dawn on Monday, 16th July, the darkness of the New Mexico desert became light as a ball of fire many times more brilliant than the sun rose into the still air. Oppenheimer recalled that at the time "a few people laughed and a few people cried. Most people were silent."

The sound of the mighty explosion came minutes after the fireball erupted. The observers who watched the bomb from their shelter many miles away were satisfied that America had now found the weapon that could win the war.

The Alamogordo test: a fireball erupts in the desert darkness.

Was the bomb needed to end the war with Japan?

The Japanese had followed up their attack on the American fleet at Pearl Harbor with a string of rapid and almost unopposed conquests of British and American colonies in the Pacific. In the first hundred days Japan overran Hong Kong, the Philippines, the Marianas, Wake Island, the Marshall and Gilbert Islands, Malaya, Burma and the Dutch East Indies. Thereafter the tide of Japanese victories began to turn. The Battle of the Coral Sea, from 6th-8th May, 1942, fought between Japanese and American carrier-based aircraft off the coast of New Guinea, averted the Japanese threat to Australia. On 4th June, 1942, at the Battle of Midway, the American fleet won a decisive naval victory, sinking Japan's four largest aircraft carriers in an operation carried out by aircraft from the US carrier, *Yorktown*.

From mid-1943 Japan's hold on her newly won territories began to weaken. American marines gradually conquered one Pacific island group after another, while other Allied troops advanced in New Guinea and landed in the Philippines. Japan's airforce and navy were effectively destroyed and the Allies pressed inexorably on towards the Japanese home islands. Here, as elsewhere, Japanese troops were prepared to fight to the last man rather than surrender. The battle for the island of Okinawa lasted from 1st April to 2nd July. A concentrated attack by Japanese suicide pilots, the *Kamikaze*, sank two US destroyers and four transport

US forces unload supplies on Iwojima, captured from the Japanese at the end of March 1945. The island was only 750 miles from Tokyo, and its capture enabled the Americans to intensify their air-raids on the Japanese mainland.

ships on 6th April. They also inflicted much damage. Of a total of 355 suicide planes, only 24 actually hit their targets.

Meanwhile, on the Japanese home islands, where an American invasion was feared, women, children and old people were trained to use bamboo spears and other home-made weapons. If American troops had invaded Japan there would certainly have been enormous losses on both sides.

Air raids on Japan

The bombing of Hiroshima and Nagasaki was presented by Truman and his advisers as an alternative to invasion, the lesser of two evils. But, while there is some truth in this argument, there is evidence that bombardment of Japanese cities by the US airforce had already brought Japan to the verge of surrender.

As early as July 1944, B29s had carried out bombing raids against Japan from bases in India. Airfields on Saipan, Guam and Tinian were built in the wake of the successful capture of the Marianas from the Japanese. On 21st November, 1944, the first B29 bomber raid was launched from there. From March 1945, as all airfields became fully operational, over 139,000 tonnes of bombs rained down on Japanese cities. In addition, B29s laid minefields around Japan's main ports, effectively cutting off her sea trade – particularly her vital imports of fuel oil.

Perhaps the most devastating raid of all was the incendiary raid on Tokyo on the night of 9th March, 1945. 334 B29s from Guam and Tinian took part in this low-level raid. As the bombers flew over the city they dropped clusters of bombs filled with napalm jelly. Exploding in mid-air, the bombs rained down liquid fire on the city below. The effect was an

Bomb damage after the incendiary raid on Tokyo.

uncontrollable fire storm. The heat from thousands of separate fires created currents of hot air which fanned the flames even higher. Around 125,000 people died in this raid and by the next morning 15.8 square miles of the city had been burned out. In this one raid nearly half of Japan's capital city had been utterly destroyed and over a million of the raid's survivors had been made homeless.

From the beginning of 1945 until the end of the war, sixty Japanese cities were subjected to this sort of attack. High on the list of targets were factories supplying arms and munitions. With defeat now staring them in the face, the Japanese public began to turn against their military leaders.

Political changes in Japan   In April 1945 Japan's hard-line Prime Minister was dismissed from office and replaced by the more moderate Admiral Suzuki Kantaro. As the US stepped up her bombing campaign, Kantaro's government began to look for ways to end the war without dishonour. But ending the war was no easy task. Part military and part civilian, the Japanese government was hopelessly divided. Only among Japan's military leaders was there any broad agreement – and their view was that the war should be continued, whatever the consequences. The stalemate was to have disastrous consequences for Japan. Even the Emperor had no power to overrule the government.

In May 1945, Germany, a nominal ally of Japan since September 1940, surrendered to the Allies. The war in Europe was over. Whatever hope Japan may have had of keeping her enemies at bay was likewise at an end: fresh American and British troops would now be able to fight alongside their armies in the Pacific and mount a final assault on Japan. Japan's search for a peaceful solution intensified.

The main hope lay in Japan's relationship with the Soviet Union. In the spring of 1941 the two countries had signed a non-aggression pact leaving each one free to concentrate her war efforts on fighting one major enemy – the Soviet Union against Germany and Japan against the United States.

As an ally of the United States, the Soviet Union seemed the ideal country through which to conduct peace negotiations. In May and in July 1945, Prime Minister Kantaro made repeated approaches to the Soviet foreign embassy requesting them to mediate with the United States. These requests were received with indifference. The Soviet leader, Stalin, realized that there was much to be gained by prolonging the war. A seriously weakened Japan would be unable to defend her territorial gains in Northern China against Soviet invasion.

Potsdam   In July the leaders of the Allies, Truman, Churchill and Stalin, and the Chinese leader, Chiang Kai-Shek, attended a conference at Potsdam in Germany to discuss the post-war reorganization of Europe and the progress of the war against Japan. The Russians told Truman that Japan wanted to discuss surrender terms, but he was unwilling to enter into talks with the Japanese. Like Churchill, Truman was determined to extract an unconditional surrender from them. What Truman and Churchill did not tell Stalin when they discussed Japan's position was that the United States had, on 16th July, successfully tested the world's first atom bomb. Truman referred only to a new and enormously destructive weapon.

By 26th July, the USA, Britain and China had considered Japan's desire for talks and formally announced their terms for bringing the war to an end. The Potsdam Declaration, signed by the three allies, demanded among other things the handing over of all Japan's territories overseas, the occupation of Japan by US forces and the punishment of war criminals. Acceptance of these terms was to be unconditional. Truman added a dire warning to the Declaration. If Japan did not surrender, "the only alternative . . . is prompt and utter destruction".

Japan's Prime Minister wavered. The Potsdam Declaration had made no reference to the fate of the Emperor, Hirohito. For the Americans to have punished the Emperor as a war criminal would have seemed an act not just of barbarism but of sacrilege, to the Japanese who regarded their Emperor as a divine ruler. Prime Minister Kantaro could not agree to the surrender terms until this point had been clarified. Furthermore, he was bound to consult the Emperor himself. His answer to the United States and her allies was therefore unclear and ambiguous. He did not reject the surrender terms outright; neither did he accept them. Caught between loyalty to his Emperor and the need to end the war without further bloodshed, Kantaro felt himself in an impossible position.

Truman took Kantaro's response as a gesture of defiance. He gave word to the airforce commander in the Marianas, General Spaatz, that the two available atom bombs were to be used against Japan as soon after 3rd August as possible. It is evident, therefore, that Truman did not expect the Japanese to change their minds and depose their Emperor. Further talks were ruled out. If negotiations had taken place at this stage then it is quite probable that surrender terms could have been agreed and the position of the Emperor respected.

A demonstration of power

By July 1945, the momentum of the atom bomb's development had reached a climax. Truman realized that to use it would confer political and military advantages on the United States far beyond a mere victory over Japan, already bombed into submission. In particular, the bomb would demonstrate US power to the Russians. With Japanese territories in China and the Pacific to be redistributed, and with European and world maps being redrawn, the threat of an atom bomb would surely prevent the Soviet Union from becoming too greedy and too powerful.

Truman did not consult his army commanders in the Pacific and none of these men knew of the bomb's existence until after it had been dropped. The bombing of Hiroshima was therefore not part of a co-ordinated strategy in preparation for an invasion by armed forces. But neither was it expected that the atom bomb alone would quickly bring about Japan's surrender.

With just two atom bombs at his disposal, Truman gave his airforce commander complete freedom in the choice of target and in the timing of the bombing missions. American Secretary of State, Henry Stimson made just one condition: that the ancient religious centre of Japan, Kyoto, should not be bombed.

The three days that elapsed between the bombing of Hiroshima and the bombing of Nagasaki did not allow the Japanese sufficient time to respond formally to Truman's renewed call for their unconditional surrender. Once the bombing missions had been completed, there would be nothing to prevent the discussion of surrender terms.

Why bomb Hiroshima?

If a demonstration of force had been all that was needed to bring about a swift surrender and to put the brake on the Soviet Union's territorial claims, then why was it necessary to drop the bomb on a city? Why not drop it on deserted countryside? Better still, announce the time and place of such an atom bomb drop so that Japanese leaders could witness the awesome power of the new weapon that could be used against them.

Interestingly, all of these questions were discussed at a meeting which took place at the Pentagon, the US military headquarters, on 31 May, 1945. Oppenheimer was present.

51

At the time there was some uncertainty over the bomb's effect. It might misfire. If the bomb failed to explode before an invited audience of Japanese leaders, then the US would lose face. To announce a bombing mission might also give the Japanese a chance to shoot down the bomber or to move prisoners of war into the chosen test area. The meeting unanimously decided that no warning should be given to Japan. The committee also advised that the target for the atom bomb should be a large city containing a legitimate military target such as an army base or a munitions factory. Hiroshima fitted these conditions perfectly.

In order to be able to study the effect of the atom bomb, it was also important that the city chosen should have suffered little or no previous bomb damage. The uncertain weather conditions over Japan meant that the decision over the timing of the bombing mission had to be left with the airforce commander in the Marianas. Perfect visibility was needed. There must be no risk of missing the target. Clear skies were also needed to enable the explosion to be recorded on film and for observation planes to assess the extent of the damage.

The first bomb is dropped

The atom bomb was dropped on Hiroshima at 8.15 a.m. (local time) on 6th August. Sixteen hours later Truman announced a fresh ultimatum for Japan. If she did not surrender unconditionally, Truman threatened "a rain of ruin from the air, the like of which has never been seen on this earth". Again, no mention was made of the proposed fate of the Emperor.

The government in Tokyo again seemed slow to respond, but this is not as surprising as it seems. It took twenty-four hours for the first isolated reports of the tragedy to be confirmed in the capital. On the evening of 7th August the Japanese ambassador to the Soviet Union, acting on instructions from his government, entered foreign minister Molotov's office in the Kremlin. He had come to request immediate talks with the United States. It was a plea for peace. Molotov received the request coldly. Then he informed the ambassador that, as from 8th August, the USSR herself would be at war with Japan.

On 9th August a plutonium bomb was dropped on Nagasaki. 23,753 people died. On that same day, Stalin's Red Army poured over the Russian border to capture Japanese-held Manchuria in northern China.

Peace at all costs

The situation facing the Japanese government was desperate.

The government needed to but could not agree unanimously to accept the terms of the Potsdam Declaration. Emperor Hirohito acted to break the deadlock. In the early hours of 10th August he summoned the entire government to his underground living quarters beneath his bomb-damaged palace in Tokyo. Urging them to accept defeat and to ask for an immediate armistice after which surrender terms could be negotiated, he asked each minister to sign a carefully prepared statement to this effect. By dawn, every minister had signed. The news was sent immediately to Japanese embassies in Sweden and Switzerland, where it was relayed to the Allied leaders.

As negotiations began, Truman ordered all bombing raids on Japan to cease. By 14th August final details had still not been agreed. Truman gave his airforce the order to recommence bombing. One final mission was flown over Japan. Before the last B29 had returned to base, Japan had agreed to an unconditional surrender. The time was noon and the date 15th August, 1945.

President Harry S. Truman announces Japan's surrender at a White House press conference, 15th August, 1945.

The effect of the bomb on Hiroshima

The death toll at Hiroshima is widely given as 140,000, but this figure represents only the deaths up to December 1945. In a nuclear explosion, only a certain number of people die immediately, as a result of blast injuries or burns. Many more will die from being exposed to the invisible killer – radiation.

Near the centre of the blast, people received high doses of radiation and died within hours or days. But radiation can be

53

spread over a wide area as fallout – the dust and debris of a nuclear explosion. It can also remain active for a long time. Some radiation victims lived outside Hiroshima. Some were people who had come to the stricken city to help rescue survivors.

Radiation alters the structure of cells within the human body, causing diseases such as leukemia and cancer. Children born to pregnant women exposed to high doses of radio-activity may be mentally retarded or handicapped. For various reasons, many of these effects are delayed and, even today, people in Japan are dying as a result of the Hiroshima bomb.

Surveys have revealed that up to the end of 1945 approximately 140,000 people had died as a result of exposure to the atomic bomb. Five years later that figure had risen to 200,000. Today no-one can be sure of the exact figure for premature deaths resulting from exposure to radiation, but it is thought to run into thousands. If the Hiroshima death toll were revised to include premature deaths related to radiation that have occurred since December 1945 then the figure might well be almost double.

General Douglas MacArthur and Emperor Hirohito at the American Embassy in Tokyo, September 1945. It was the first time in history that a Japanese ruler had left his palace to visit a foreigner.

Hiroshima fire station destroyed by the atom blast.

And the atom bomb that destroyed Hiroshima did not just kill tens of thousands of people; it killed a community as well. The surviving civilian population was homeless. Families were split up and all suffered the loss of at least one of their members. Local government ceased to function and, with it, important organizations such as the fire brigade, police, schools and medical services. There was no immediate programme of aid to look after survivors and, indeed, no money with which to treat the sick and wounded or to repair the damage to property. People had to help themselves.

Early medical help for victims of the bombing was inadequate and so many died who might otherwise have been saved. With no medical supplies, burns victims were treated with cooking oil or even machine oil. Open wounds festered

55

and turned gangrenous because there was not enough disinfectant to cleanse them. Food shortages left patients too weak to recover from their injuries and many died as a result. The arrival of the American occupation forces and the International Red Cross brought much needed medical aid. Slowly the city was rebuilt and, by the end of 1950, Hiroshima had thirty-five hospitals.

In the 1951 San Francisco Peace Treaty, signed by the USA and Japan, Japan agreed not to press for future compensation for her bomb victims. Better medical care and free treatment now exist in Japan for the victims of Hiroshima. But for a long while they were forced to depend on charities and on the international fund-raising activities of peace movements.

Hiroshima rises from the ruins. Seven months after the bomb, citizens begin to rebuild their lives.

How did the post-war arms race come about?

"If atomic bombs are to be added to the arsenals of a warring world, then the time will come when mankind will curse the name of Los Alamos and Hiroshima.

The peoples of the world must unite or they will perish . . . ."

Surprisingly, these are not the words of an anti-nuclear campaigner. They were spoken by J. Robert Oppenheimer in a farewell speech to his colleagues at Los Alamos, from which he resigned as director on 16th October, 1945. Oppenheimer warned that other countries would develop their own nuclear weapons and that this would lead to a dangerous and possibly destructive arms race unless international agreement were reached.

However, it was not simply the manufacture of nuclear weapons that was seen as a threat to world peace. The peacetime application of nuclear power itself became an issue of international importance. The process of generating power in a nuclear reactor led to the formation of plutonium – the raw material from which bombs could be made. It was thus impossible to restrict nuclear power to providing cheap energy. If a country possessed the means to generate energy from a nuclear reactor, then it could also make an atom bomb.

The UN Atomic Energy Commission At the United Nations assembly, the United States proposed that an international body be set up to control all future world developments of nuclear energy. So, on 24th January, 1946, the United Nations Atomic Energy Commission was born. Among its aims was "the elimination from national armaments of atomic weapons and of all other major weapons adaptable to mass destruction".

On 14th June, 1946, the United States put forward a proposal to the Commission calling for the international control of nuclear power. The Baruch Plan, named after the politician who led the US delegation, proposed that no country should be able to develop nuclear energy in future without the Commission's approval. The Plan also suggested, however, that no one country should be able to block a decision reached by the Commission by voting against the majority. Since most countries represented on the Commission were sympathetic to the United States, the

Soviet Union believed that the United States would not only prevent her from developing nuclear weapons but also deny her the opportunity of rebuilding her former industrial strength with the aid of cheap nuclear power. As a lone voice at the United Nations, the Soviet Union would be denied the right to vote against proposals that were against her own interests.

The Soviet Union put forward a counter-proposal on 19th June that all atomic weapons be banned and those already in existence destroyed. While the United Nations debated, the United States announced the start of a series of atomic weapons tests in the Pacific. In spite of her warlike stance, the United States' proposal attracted the support of a large majority of countries represented at the United Nations, most of them allies or dependants of the USA.

The Soviet Union builds her own bomb

In rejecting the Soviet plan, the United Nations may well have lost the only real chance it has ever been given to avoid a nuclear arms race. The Soviet Union felt that her security and her future position as an international power were threatened by the United States' possession of the atom bomb. In spite of the UN Resolution, the Soviet Union considered that she had no choice but to compete with the United States on equal terms.

The exploding of a nuclear device within the Soviet Union was detected by US planes monitoring levels of radioactivity near the East German border in September 1949. Despite silence from the Soviet Union, President Truman announced the atom bomb test to the world that same month. The news came as a considerable shock to political leaders in the States and in Britain. No one had expected Soviet scientists to build a bomb within such a short time. The tension that already existed between the Soviet Union and her former allies in Europe and in Korea was heightened and many politicians forecast war.

Weapons testing

On 31st January, 1950, President Truman authorized work to go ahead on the hydrogen bomb that scientists at Los Alamos had begun to develop during the last years of the Second World War. The hydrogen bomb worked on the principle of fusing atoms together rather than splitting them. Fusion released many times more energy than a nuclear chain reaction. But to fuse atoms demanded a burst of enormously high temperature. An atomic explosion created this high temperature and triggered the much larger secondary explosion caused by the fusion of hydrogen atoms.

Meanwhile, in Britain, Prime Minister Clement Attlee pushed ahead with a secret British atom bomb project. On 3rd October, 1952, Britain exploded her first atom bomb at Monte Bello. Less than a month later, the United States tested her first H-bomb at Eniwetok Atoll in the Pacific. The explosive power of that first hydrogen bomb was estimated to be the equivalent of ten million tonnes of TNT (ten megatons) – 700 times as powerful as the Hiroshima bomb!

The 1950s saw a speeding up of the arms race. First the Soviet Union and then Britain tested their own hydrogen bombs. France, too, joined the nuclear nations.

But nuclear weapons tests, besides demonstrating the superiority of one nation's technology over another's, demonstrated the fragility of life on earth. The H-bomb was so powerful that millions of people could be killed in one explosion and whole areas of the earth's surface could be rendered uninhabitable.

The American H-bomb test at Bikini Atoll in March 1954 produced an explosion of 15 megatons – almost twice as great as had been forecast. 100 miles away, radioactive fallout rained down upon a Japanese fishing boat, the *Lucky Dragon*. One member of the crew died and others suffered from radiation sickness.

All over the world, public opinion moved against nuclear weapons. Anti-nuclear protest movements sprang up in Japan and in other countries. In Britain, protest movements joined forces to form the Committee for National Disarmament (CND) early in 1958. Led by Bertrand Russell, CND supporters marched on the government's weapons research centre at Aldermaston, Berkshire.

The first H-bomb explosion.

The nuclear arms race speeds up

In spite of protest movements, stockpiles of nuclear weapons continued to rise and weapons became more deadly and more accurate. In the early 1950s nuclear warheads existed in the form of bombs which had to be dropped by aircraft. But when the Russians launched Sputnik, the world's first orbiting satellite, on 4th October, 1957, many ideas about nuclear warfare changed. If a rocket could be made powerful enough to launch a satellite into orbit around the earth, then that same rocket on a different trajectory could deliver a nuclear warhead from one continent to another. Inter-continental ballistic missiles (ICBMs) capable of being accurately targeted were developed by both the Soviet Union and the United States. These completely eliminated the risk and uncertainty of a conventional bomber attack which, in any case, took far longer to reach its target.

The superpowers (the Soviet Union and the USA) now tried to build enough missiles to cover the main military, civilian and industrial targets in each other's countries. A vast, under-populated country, the Soviet Union had the advantage since it would clearly take more American warheads to completely destroy all her many centres of population and industry. In the race to build ICBMs the winner would be the side that had the greater number of missiles.

The nuclear deterrent

It was evident that in a nuclear war there could be no winner – only losers. Early warning of a nuclear attack against either the US or the USSR would prompt a devastating counter-attack. Whole cities would be destroyed in the exchange of missiles and areas of countryside turned into arid, radioactive deserts.

Military planners on both sides, however, claimed to believe that the object of building up stockpiles of nuclear weapons was to *deter* an enemy from declaring war on them and from attacking their country with either nuclear or conventional weapons. To be effective, the deterrent must keep changing to match the latest advances in weapon technology.

In the late 1950s, as the Soviets developed missiles that could be targeted with pinpoint accuracy, so the United States went to a great deal of trouble to develop missiles that could be moved by transporter in times of international crisis. At the same time they built a fleet of missile-carrying submarines capable of launching a nuclear attack from beneath the waves. A stalemate in which neither side possessed the advantage could have continued indefinitely had it not been for the development of the anti-ballistic missile or ABM. Capable of tracking and destroying an enemy missile before it can reach its target, ABMs give a big military advantage to whoever possesses them. America began to build up an ABM system in 1967.

Arms limitation treaties

By the late 1960s, the two superpowers were preoccupied with building arsenals of defensive ABMs in an accelerating new arms race. Each side was looking for gaps in the other's defences. But reason slowly began to prevail. With the landing of the first men on the moon in 1967 came the realization that space could quickly become the next nuclear frontier. In that same year the Americans, the Russians and fifty-eight other nations signed a treaty banning nuclear weapons from the moon and from orbiting satellites.

The Trident D-5 submarine-launched missile has a range of 6,000 miles. It can carry up to fourteen independently targeted warheads, each one with a greater explosive power than the Hiroshima bomb.

May 1972 saw the signing of the first Strategic Arms Limitation Treaty (SALT I) between the United States and the Soviet Union. In addition to limiting the numbers of inter-continental ballistic missiles (ICBMs) and submarine-launched ballistic missiles (SLBMs) the treaty restricted the numbers of defensive ABMs. Each side could deploy only 100 ABMs for the defence of cities and another 100 to defend missile sites. In 1974 these numbers were halved.

SALT I gave both sides the freedom to use spy satellites to photograph ground installations and hence check that the treaty was being honoured. Disappointingly, however, the treaty did not cover the use of a new development in nuclear weapons technology – multiple warheads. Whereas, before, a missile had only been able to carry a single warhead, now, that same missile could be adapted to carry a number of separate warheads, each of which could be programmed to hit an independent target. Ironically, while the numbers of missiles were reduced during the lifespan of the SALT I treaty, both the USA and the USSR were able to more than double their numbers of nuclear warheads.

Negotiations between the two countries continued and in June 1979 President Carter and President Brezhnev signed the SALT II Treaty. SALT II was a much less effective curb on the nuclear arms race than its predecessor. Each side was allowed 1,200 long-range missiles with multiple warheads and up to 2,250 shorter-range tactical weapons. The USA and the USSR, additionally, were free to conduct weapons research and to update their aging missile systems. Thus, the United States began research into the possibility of an entirely new

61

defensive system in which high-energy laser beams fired from earth and reflected by a network of orbiting satellites could be targeted to destroy incoming missiles. This system, the Strategic Defence Initiative (SDI) – better known as "Star Wars", is not expected to be operational until the late 1990s.

Shortly after the signing of SALT II, the Soviet Union invaded Afghanistan. As a direct response, the US Senate refused to ratify the treaty. In spite of the Senate's official rejection of the treaty, the terms agreed by Carter and Brezhnev were obeyed by both sides for many years. Under those terms the USA was able to introduce the new submarine-launched, multiple-warhead Trident missile system in 1981. Two new land-based missile systems, the long-range Pershing missile and the shorter-range Cruise missile, followed soon after. Intended for deployment in Europe, the first Cruise missile to arrive in Britain was delivered to the United States Airforce base at Greenham Common in Berkshire in November 1983.

Since the SALT II Treaty, attempts to reach agreement over arms limitation have failed. President Reagan and Mr Gorbachev met for talks at Geneva in November 1985 and at Reykjavik in October 1986. Each time the reason for the breakdown in negotiations was claimed by the Soviet leader to be the United States' refusal to abandon its "Star Wars" programme. According to Soviet politicians, "Star Wars" is not a purely defensive system; it could become a weapon of

1986: a demonstration against nuclear weapons, in front of the Industry Promotion Centre, Hiroshima.

attack. This, of course, would be in violation of an international treaty banning all weapons in space. Since Reykjavik the USA has broken the SALT II Treaty and deliberately escalated the arms race by building more Cruise missiles.

The nuclear future Today eight countries possess nuclear weapons – the United States, the Soviet Union, Britain, France, China, India, Israel and South Africa.

In a speech in 1980, Queen Elizabeth II said of nuclear weapons that "their awesome destructive power has preserved the world from major war for the past 35 years". So far, nuclear weapons have served as a deterrent. But for the bomb to remain a threat, politicians must be seen to be prepared to use it.

There have been no winners in the nuclear arms race. What happened at Hiroshima should serve to remind the world of the nightmarish consequences of nuclear war. If the memory of that city's suffering will prevent a future Armageddon, then the children of Hiroshima will not have died in vain.

Further reading

THE EVENTS

Virginia Alexandria, *Japan at War*, Time-Life, 1981
John Hersey, *Hiroshima*, Penguin Books, 1972
Publishing Committee for the Children of Hiroshima, *Children of Hiroshima*, Taylor and Francis, 1980
Hiroshima Nagasaki, Hiroshima Nagasaki Publishing Committee, 1978
The Youth Division of Soka Gakkei, *Cries for Peace*, The Japan Times Ltd, 1974
Keith Wheeler, *The Fall of Japan*, Time-Life Books, 1983

THE INVESTIGATION

Steve Birdsall, *The Saga of the Superfortress*, Sidgwick and Jackson, 1981
Nigel Calder, *Nuclear Nightmares: an investigation into possible wars*, BBC, 1979
Duncan Campbell, *War Plan UK*, Burnett Books, 1982
Ronald W. Clark, *The Greatest Power on Earth*, Sidgwick and Jackson, 1980
Peter Goodchild, *Oppenheimer, Shatterer of Worlds*, BBC, 1980
Michael Sheehan, *The Arms Race*, Martin Robertson, 1983
E.P. Thompson, *Zero Option*, Merlin Press, 1982

Index